Spot the Reindeer at Christmas

Krina Patel & Tasha Percy

Illustrated by

Marc Mones

QED
QED Publishing

It's Christmas!

There's lots to see. Come and have a look!

Ice-skating

Christmas tree

Santa's workshop

Christmas Eve

Australian Christmas

Reindeer

Christmas characters

Snow day

Christmas Day

This baby reindeer is hiding inside the book. Can you find him in every scene?

Figure skating is a type of ice-skating that includes dance moves, spins and jumps.

Can you spot these things?

yellow present   cape   red skates   tutu   puppy

Can you spot these things?

ballet shoes · spanner · blue pencil · marbles · football

Santa's elves are known by different names around the world. In Iceland they are called 'Yule Lads'.

Christmas trees were traditionally decorated with food like apples, nuts and dates.

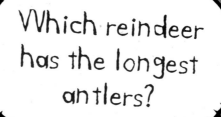

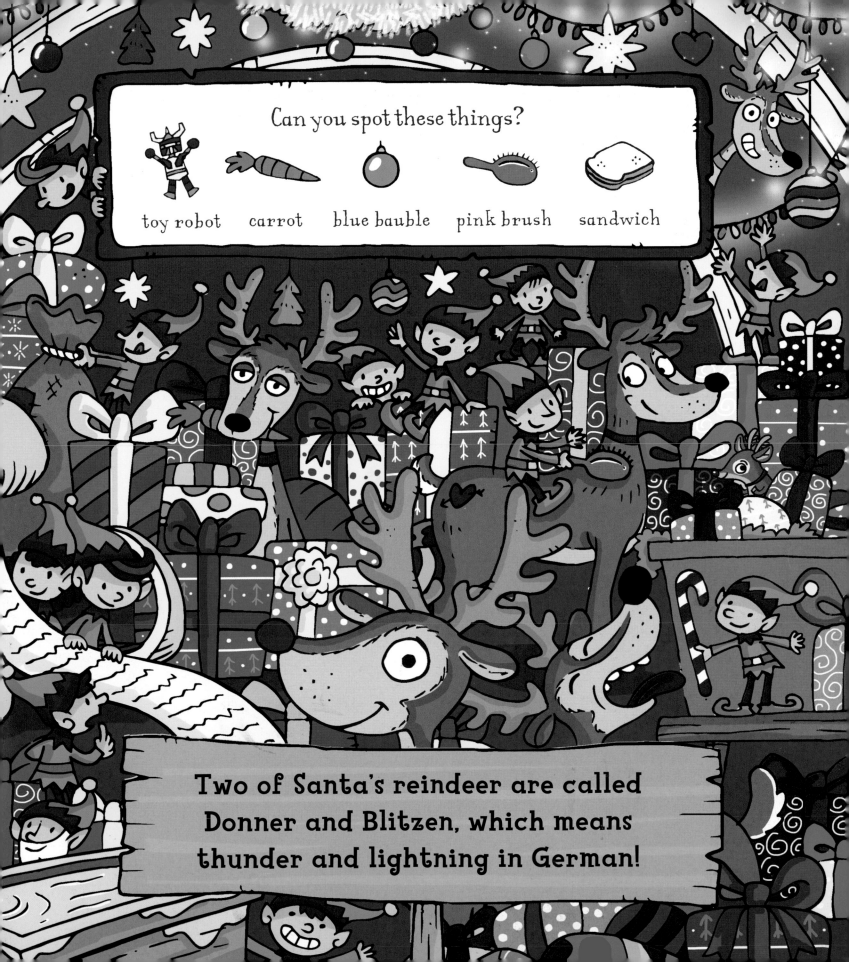

Can you spot these things?

toy robot carrot blue bauble pink brush sandwich

Two of Santa's reindeer are called Donner and Blitzen, which means thunder and lightning in German!

Gold chocolate coins are given at Christmas because St Nicholas (or Santa Claus) was said to give bags of gold coins to the poor.

Can you spot these things?

pink slippers   spotty hat   red candle   guitar   holly wreath

The carol *Silent Night* was first sung on Christmas Eve nearly 200 years ago.

In Australia, Christmas is during the summer and some families celebrate with a barbeque at the beach.

Can you spot these things?

 green flip-flops

 beach ball

crab

 mistletoe

 red cracker

Different countries have their own traditional Christmas meals including fish, goose and even octopus.

The biggest snow woman ever built was as tall as nine elephants stood on top of each other - that's 37 metres!

Can you spot these things?

snow dog   green mittens   igloo

twins   Santa hat

More to spot
Go back and find these scenes in the book!

Did you find me?

Did you Know?

Santa has nine reindeer. Their names are Dasher, Dancer, Prancer, Vixen, Comet, Cupid, Donner, Blitzen and Rudolph (the red-nosed reindeer).

Santa is known by different names around the world – such as Kanakaloka in Hawaii, Père Noël in France and Grandfather Frost in Russia.

Jingle Bells was the first song broadcast from space. It was played by the crew of the Gemini 6 mission in 1965.

If you received all the gifts from the song The Twelve Days of Christmas you would have 364 gifts!

Tinsel was once made of real silver! It was invented in Germany in 1610.

More Christmas fun!

Festive memory game

Ask an adult to help you. Arrange around ten Christmas items on a tray; you could use different decorations and ornaments. Spend a minute memorising the objects, then cover with a tea towel. How many can you remember?

Hide and seek

Choose a cuddly toy to hide around your home for a friend or family member to find, just like the reindeer in the book! You could hide other objects and make a list of things to find.

Paper plate snowman

Overlap two white paper plates, one bigger than the other, and stick them together to make the head and body. Use coloured paper, pipe cleaners and buttons to make the face, arms and accessories. You could even add glitter!

Collage Christmas tree

Cut out three different sized green paper triangles. Then stick one above the other with the smallest at the top and largest at the bottom. Decorate with coloured pens and gems. Add thread to the top to hang it up.

Designer: Krina Patel
Design Assistant: Anya Paul
Editor: Tasha Percy
Editorial Director: Victoria Garrard
Art Director: Laura Roberts-Jensen

Copyright © QED Publishing 2014

First published in the UK in 2014 by
QED Publishing
A Quarto Group company
The Old Brewery,
6 Blundell Street,
London, N7 9BH

www.qed-publishing.co.uk

A catalogue record for this book is available from the British Library.

ISBN 978 1 78171 572 7

Printed in China